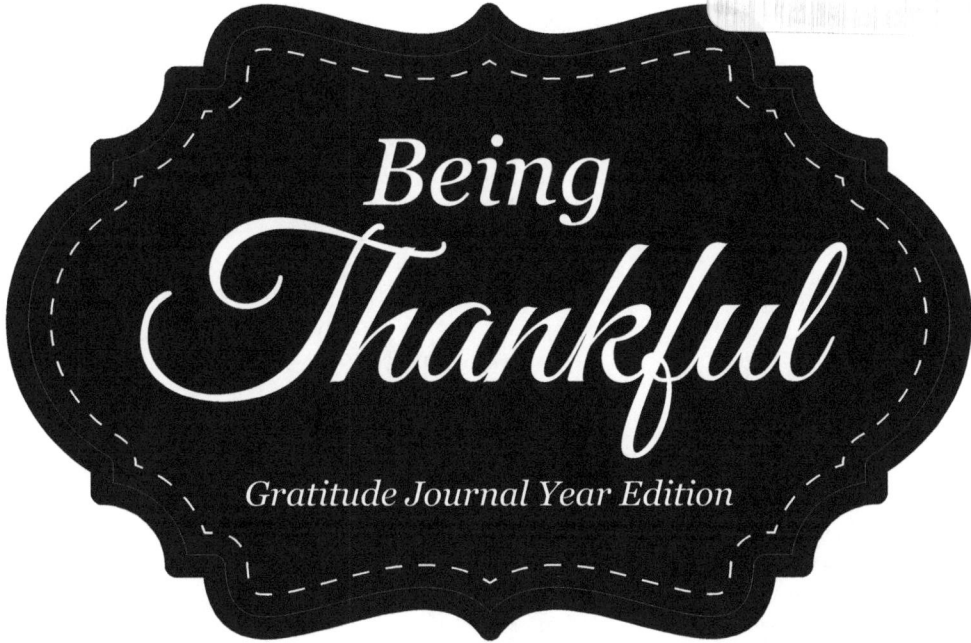

Being Thankful

Gratitude Journal Year Edition

ACTIVINOTES

Activinotes

DAILY JOURNALS, PLANNERS, NOTEBOOKS AND OTHER BLANK BOOKS

This Book Belongs To

_____

JANUARY

DATE: / / TIME: from to

Type of Practice: _____

Location: _____

Environment: _____

Feelings & Perceptions

_____

_____

_____

_____

_____

_____

_____

_____

_____

_____

_____

Insights & Realizations

_____

_____

_____

_____

_____

_____

_____

_____

_____

_____

_____

_____

Today is _____

Words	Actions

TODAY IS THE DAY

PRIORITIES

GOALS

EXTRAS

SCHEDULE

GET STUFF DONE!

MORNING

☐ _____
☐ _____
☐ _____
☐ _____
☐ _____
☐ _____

AFTERNOON

☐ _____
☐ _____
☐ _____
☐ _____
☐ _____
☐ _____

EVENING

☐ _____
☐ _____
☐ _____
☐ _____
☐ _____
☐ _____

NOTES

_____
_____
_____
_____
_____
_____
_____

FEBRUARY

DATE: / /   **TIME:** from   to

Type of Practice: _____

Location: _____

Environment: _____

Feelings & Perceptions

_____
_____
_____
_____
_____
_____
_____
_____
_____
_____
_____

Insights & Realizations

_____
_____
_____
_____
_____
_____
_____
_____
_____
_____
_____
_____

Today is _____

Words	Actions

TODAY IS THE DAY

PRIORITIES

GOALS

EXTRAS

SCHEDULE

GET STUFF DONE!

MORNING

- [ ] _____
- [ ] _____
- [ ] _____
- [ ] _____
- [ ] _____
- [ ] _____

AFTERNOON

- [ ] _____
- [ ] _____
- [ ] _____
- [ ] _____
- [ ] _____
- [ ] _____

EVENING

- [ ] _____
- [ ] _____
- [ ] _____
- [ ] _____
- [ ] _____
- [ ] _____

NOTES

_____
_____
_____
_____
_____
_____
_____

MARCH

DATE: / /

TIME: from to

Type of Practice: _____

Location: _____

Environment: _____

Feelings & Perceptions

_____
_____
_____
_____
_____
_____
_____
_____
_____
_____

Insights & Realizations

_____
_____
_____
_____
_____
_____
_____
_____
_____
_____

Today is _____

Words	Actions

TODAY IS THE DAY

PRIORITIES

GOALS

EXTRAS

SCHEDULE

GET STUFF DONE!

MORNING

☐ _____
☐ _____
☐ _____
☐ _____
☐ _____
☐ _____

AFTERNOON

☐ _____
☐ _____
☐ _____
☐ _____
☐ _____
☐ _____

EVENING

☐ _____
☐ _____
☐ _____
☐ _____
☐ _____
☐ _____

NOTES

_____
_____
_____
_____
_____
_____
_____

APRIL

DATE: / /   **TIME:** from   to

Type of Practice: _____

Location: _____

Environment: _____

Feelings & Perceptions

_____
_____
_____
_____
_____
_____
_____
_____
_____
_____

Insights & Realizations

_____
_____
_____
_____
_____
_____
_____
_____
_____
_____
_____
_____

Today is _____

Words	Actions

TODAY IS THE DAY

PRIORITIES

GOALS

EXTRAS

SCHEDULE

GET STUFF DONE!

MORNING

- ☐ _____
- ☐ _____
- ☐ _____
- ☐ _____
- ☐ _____
- ☐ _____

AFTERNOON

- ☐ _____
- ☐ _____
- ☐ _____
- ☐ _____
- ☐ _____
- ☐ _____

EVENING

- ☐ _____
- ☐ _____
- ☐ _____
- ☐ _____
- ☐ _____
- ☐ _____

NOTES

_____
_____
_____
_____
_____
_____
_____

MAY

DATE: /   /   **TIME:** from   to

Type of Practice: _____

Location: _____

Environment: _____

Feelings & Perceptions

_____
_____
_____
_____
_____
_____
_____
_____
_____
_____
_____

Insights & Realizations

_____
_____
_____
_____
_____
_____
_____
_____
_____
_____

Today is _____

Words	Actions

TODAY IS THE DAY

PRIORITIES

GOALS

EXTRAS

SCHEDULE

GET STUFF DONE!

MORNING

☐ _____
☐ _____
☐ _____
☐ _____
☐ _____
☐ _____

AFTERNOON

☐ _____
☐ _____
☐ _____
☐ _____
☐ _____
☐ _____

EVENING

☐ _____
☐ _____
☐ _____
☐ _____
☐ _____
☐ _____

NOTES

_____
_____
_____
_____
_____
_____
_____

JUNE

DATE: / /

TIME: from   to

Type of Practice: _____

Location: _____

Environment: _____

Feelings & Perceptions

_____

_____

_____

_____

_____

_____

_____

_____

_____

_____

Insights & Realizations

_____

_____

_____

_____

_____

_____

_____

_____

_____

_____

_____

Today is _____

Words	Actions

TODAY IS THE DAY

PRIORITIES

SCHEDULE

GOALS

EXTRAS

GET STUFF DONE!

MORNING

- ☐ _____
- ☐ _____
- ☐ _____
- ☐ _____
- ☐ _____
- ☐ _____

AFTERNOON

- ☐ _____
- ☐ _____
- ☐ _____
- ☐ _____
- ☐ _____
- ☐ _____

EVENING

- ☐ _____
- ☐ _____
- ☐ _____
- ☐ _____
- ☐ _____
- ☐ _____

NOTES

_____
_____
_____
_____
_____
_____
_____

JULY

DATE: / /

TIME: from to

Type of Practice: _____

Location: _____

Environment: _____

Feelings & Perceptions

_____
_____
_____
_____
_____
_____
_____
_____
_____
_____

Insights & Realizations

_____
_____
_____
_____
_____
_____
_____
_____
_____
_____

Today is _____

Words	Actions

TODAY IS THE DAY

PRIORITIES

SCHEDULE

GOALS

EXTRAS

GET STUFF DONE!

MORNING

☐ _____
☐ _____
☐ _____
☐ _____
☐ _____
☐ _____

AFTERNOON

☐ _____
☐ _____
☐ _____
☐ _____
☐ _____
☐ _____

EVENING

☐ _____
☐ _____
☐ _____
☐ _____
☐ _____
☐ _____

NOTES

_____
_____
_____
_____
_____
_____
_____

AUGUST

DATE: / /   **TIME:** from   to

Type of Practice: _____

Location: _____

Environment: _____

Feelings & Perceptions

_____
_____
_____
_____
_____
_____
_____
_____
_____
_____

Insights & Realizations

_____
_____
_____
_____
_____
_____
_____
_____
_____
_____
_____

Today is _____

Words	Actions

TODAY IS THE DAY

PRIORITIES

GOALS

EXTRAS

SCHEDULE

GET STUFF DONE!

MORNING

☐ _____
☐ _____
☐ _____
☐ _____
☐ _____
☐ _____

AFTERNOON

☐ _____
☐ _____
☐ _____
☐ _____
☐ _____
☐ _____

EVENING

☐ _____
☐ _____
☐ _____
☐ _____
☐ _____
☐ _____

NOTES

_____
_____
_____
_____
_____
_____
_____

SEPTEMBER

DATE: / /　　　**TIME:** from　　　to

Type of Practice: _____

Location: _____

Environment: _____

Feelings & Perceptions

_____
_____
_____
_____
_____
_____
_____
_____
_____
_____

Insights & Realizations

_____
_____
_____
_____
_____
_____
_____
_____
_____
_____
_____
_____

Today is _____

Words	Actions

TODAY IS THE DAY

PRIORITIES

GOALS

EXTRAS

SCHEDULE

GET STUFF DONE!

MORNING

☐ _____
☐ _____
☐ _____
☐ _____
☐ _____
☐ _____

AFTERNOON

☐ _____
☐ _____
☐ _____
☐ _____
☐ _____
☐ _____

EVENING

☐ _____
☐ _____
☐ _____
☐ _____
☐ _____
☐ _____

NOTES

_____
_____
_____
_____
_____
_____
_____

OCTOBER

DATE: /   /   TIME: from   to

Type of Practice: _____

Location: _____

Environment: _____

Feelings & Perceptions

_____
_____
_____
_____
_____
_____
_____
_____
_____
_____

Insights & Realizations

_____
_____
_____
_____
_____
_____
_____
_____
_____
_____
_____

Today is _____

Words	Actions

TODAY IS THE DAY

PRIORITIES

GOALS

EXTRAS

SCHEDULE

GET STUFF DONE!

MORNING

☐ _____
☐ _____
☐ _____
☐ _____
☐ _____
☐ _____

AFTERNOON

☐ _____
☐ _____
☐ _____
☐ _____
☐ _____
☐ _____

EVENING

☐ _____
☐ _____
☐ _____
☐ _____
☐ _____
☐ _____

NOTES

_____
_____
_____
_____
_____
_____
_____

NOVEMBER

DATE: /   /

TIME: from   to

Type of Practice: _____

Location: _____

Environment: _____

Feelings & Perceptions

_____

_____

_____

_____

_____

_____

_____

_____

_____

_____

Insights & Realizations

_____

_____

_____

_____

_____

_____

_____

_____

_____

_____

_____

Today is _____

Words	Actions

TODAY IS THE DAY

PRIORITIES

GOALS

EXTRAS

SCHEDULE

GET STUFF DONE!

MORNING

- ☐ _____
- ☐ _____
- ☐ _____
- ☐ _____
- ☐ _____
- ☐ _____

AFTERNOON

- ☐ _____
- ☐ _____
- ☐ _____
- ☐ _____
- ☐ _____
- ☐ _____

EVENING

- ☐ _____
- ☐ _____
- ☐ _____
- ☐ _____
- ☐ _____
- ☐ _____

NOTES

_____
_____
_____
_____
_____
_____
_____

DECEMBER

DATE: / /   **TIME:** from   to

Type of Practice: _____

Location: _____

Environment: _____

Feelings & Perceptions

_____
_____
_____
_____
_____
_____
_____
_____
_____
_____
_____

Insights & Realizations

_____
_____
_____
_____
_____
_____
_____
_____
_____
_____
_____

Today is _____

Words	Actions

TODAY IS THE DAY

PRIORITIES

GOALS

EXTRAS

SCHEDULE

GET STUFF DONE!

MORNING

- [ ] _____
- [ ] _____
- [ ] _____
- [ ] _____
- [ ] _____
- [ ] _____

AFTERNOON

- [ ] _____
- [ ] _____
- [ ] _____
- [ ] _____
- [ ] _____
- [ ] _____

EVENING

- [ ] _____
- [ ] _____
- [ ] _____
- [ ] _____
- [ ] _____
- [ ] _____

NOTES

_____
_____
_____
_____
_____
_____
_____

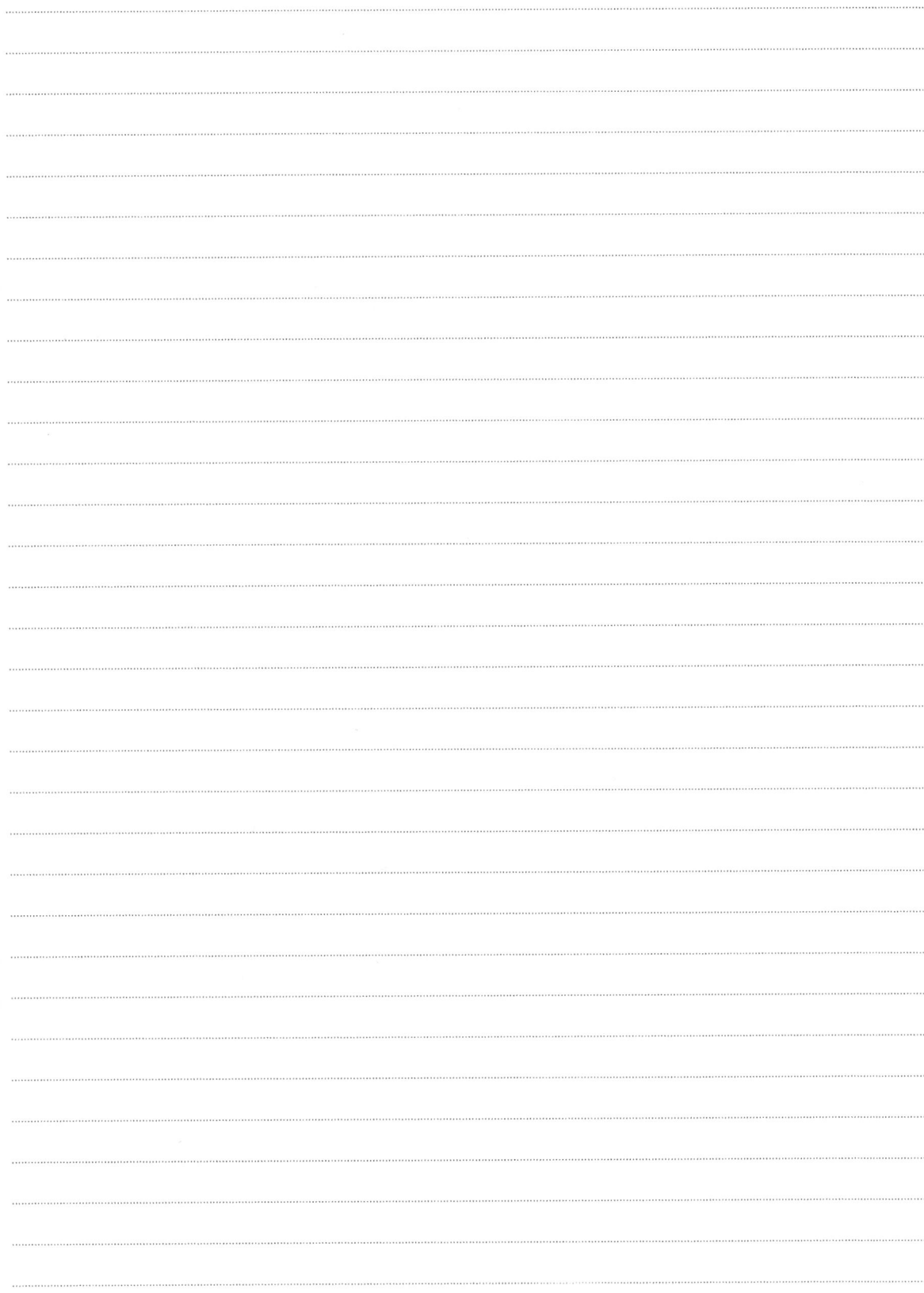

www.ingramcontent.com/pod-product-compliance
Lightning Source LLC
Chambersburg PA
CBHW081333090426
42737CB00017B/3126